DISASTERS IN HISTORY

THE SCHOOLCHILDREN'S
BLIZZARD

by Donald B. Lemke
illustrated by Dave Hoover,
Richard Dominguez,
and Charles Barnett III

Consultant:
David Laskin, author
The Children's Blizzard

Capstone
press®

Mankato, Minnesota

Graphic Library is published by Capstone Press,
151 Good Counsel Drive, P.O. Box 669, Mankato, Minnesota 56002.
www.capstonepress.com

1 2 3 4 5 6 12 11 10 09 08 07

Library of Congress Cataloging-in-Publication Data
Lemke, Donald B.
    The schoolchildren's blizzard / by Donald B. Lemke; illustrated by Dave Hoover,
Richard Dominguez, and Charles Barnett III.
    p. cm. —(Graphic library. Disasters in history)
    Summary: "In graphic novel format, tells the gripping story of the devastating 1888
blizzard that suddenly exploded across the Great Plains, killing hundreds of children as they
walked home from school"—Provided by publisher.
    Includes bibliographical references and index.
    ISBN-13: 978-1-4296-0157-3 (hardcover)
    ISBN-10: 1-4296-0157-4 (hardcover)
    1. Middle West—History—19th century—Juvenile literature. 2. Blizzards—Middle
West—History—19th century—Juvenile literature. 3. Prairies—Middle West—History—19th
century—Juvenile literature. 4. Children—Middle West—Death—History—19th century—
Juvenile literature. 5. Hypothermia—Middle West—History—19th century—Juvenile
literature. 6. Pioneers—Middle West—History—19th century—Juvenile literature. 7.
Immigrants—Middle West—History—19th century—Juvenile literature. 8. Frontier and
pioneer life—Middle West—Juvenile literature. 9. Graphic novels. I. Hoover, Dave, 1955–
II. Dominguez, Richard. III. Barnett, Charles, III. IV. Title. V. Series.
F595.L477 2008
977'.02—dc22   2007000259

Designers
Thomas Emery and Kim Brown

Colorist
Tami Collins

Editor
Christine Peterson

**Portions of this story are based upon archival research assembled by
David Laskin in his original narrative *The Children's Blizzard*
(New York: HarperCollins, 2004).**

TABLE OF CONTENTS

Without radios, TVs, or phones, the Knieriems and other pioneers had no way of knowing the weather beyond their horizon.

In St. Paul, Minnesota, Sergeant Patrick Lyons gathered weather data for the U.S. Signal Corps. Lyons recorded temperatures, wind speeds, and other conditions.

He used the best equipment available, including thermometers, rain gauges, and an anemometer to measure wind speed.

Lieutenant Thomas Mayhew Woodruff headed the St. Paul Signal Corps branch office.

What's the morning report, Sergeant Lyons?

Two degrees below zero at 6 o'clock. That's 23 degrees warmer than yesterday.

How about the other stations, Sergeant McAdie?

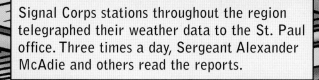

Signal Corps stations throughout the region telegraphed their weather data to the St. Paul office. Three times a day, Sergeant Alexander McAdie and others read the reports.

Nineteen degrees in Huron, Dakota. A balmy 28 degrees in North Platte, Nebraska.

What about farther west? Has Helena, Montana, reported?

Helena's temperature dropped almost 50 degrees since yesterday. They're also reporting strong winds and snow.

Let's map out the rest of these numbers. The weather's about to take a turn for the worse.

With the reports, Woodruff and McAdie made maps of the area's weather and used them to make forecasts.

CHAPTER 3

FACING THE STORM

By evening, the blizzard had moved south and east through the Midwest. Hundreds of young teachers were making the same life-or-death decision.

In Ord, Nebraska, Minnie Mae Freeman led her students to a nearby farmhouse.

With no food or fuel, others had no choice but to leave. In Plainview, Nebraska, a young teacher named Lois Royce and her three students left their schoolhouse to seek safer shelter.

Thousands of others in Minnesota, Iowa, and Nebraska struggled against the wind and snow.

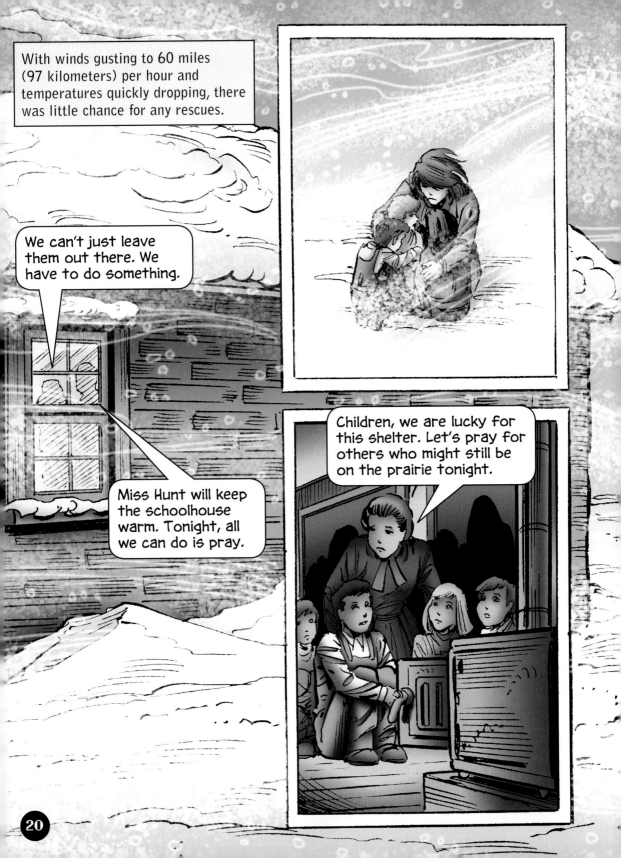

From every stormy wind that blows; From every swelling tide of woes; There is a calm, a sure retreat . . .

Back in St. Paul, Woodruff and McAdie had prepared their forecast for the following day.

For Dakota: Local snows, colder with a cold wave.

The weather would offer no relief.

As the snow melted in spring, more victims of the January 12 blizzard were found. The storm had taken the lives of nearly 500 people, including many children.

In the years to come, many pioneers in Nebraska and the Dakotas left the harsh weather of the prairie behind.

Even today, the area of the Great Plains remains much the same as in 1888.

Although advances in technology increase the ability to track storms and warn people, the fury of a winter blizzard will never be tamed.

27

MORE ABOUT THE BLIZZARD

With limited trees on the prairie, pioneers searched for other fuel sources. Some families twisted hay or straw. They burned the twists, called "cats," in stoves to keep warm. Other settlers burned corncobs or dried animal dung called "chips." These fuels were cheaper and more widely available than wood or coal.

On January 12, 1888, many young teachers led their students through the blinding storm to safety. Minnie Mae Freeman became one of the most famous teachers of the storm. She guided her students to a nearby farmhouse in Ord, Nebraska. Soon after, a song was written about her called "Thirteen were Saved, or Nebraska's Fearless Maid."

During the 1800s, many families on the Great Plains lived in houses made of sod. With few trees on the prairie, dirt and grass were the best materials available. These shelters protected pioneers against harsh weather better than wooden homes. They stayed cooler in summer and warmer in the winter. If not for the mice and snakes burrowing through the ceiling, people might still live in sod houses today.

Many people believe a large amount of snow is necessary for a blizzard. In fact, no snow is needed at all. Any storm with low temperatures, winds greater than 35 miles (56 kilometers) per hour, and reduced visibility is called a blizzard. Snow already on the ground can be picked up by wind and make it hard to see.

During the Schoolchildren's Blizzard, many people reported feeling a strange electricity and seeing sparks from metal objects. Tiny particles of snow colliding and rubbing together had filled the air with electricity. This rare weather event is sometimes known as St. Elmo's Fire.

Two months after the Schoolchildren's Blizzard, a snowstorm hit New York City. On March 12, 1888, 21 inches (53 centimeters) of snow fell in the city. With winds blowing at 75 miles (121 kilometers) per hour, the storm drifted snow, stranded residents, and caused nearly 400 deaths.

In the 2000 U.S. census, North Dakota, South Dakota, Montana, and Nebraska ranked among the least populated states in America. Harsh weather is one reason why prairie grasses and farmland still stretch to the horizon.

GLOSSARY

anemometer (an-i-MOM-uh-tur)—a scientific instrument used to measure the wind's speed

forecast (FOR-kast)—a prediction of changes in the weather

frantic (FRAN-tik)—wildly excited by worry or fear

frostbite (FRAWST-bite)—a condition that occurs when cold temperatures freeze skin

horizon (huh-RYE-zuhn)—the line where the sky and the earth or sea seem to meet

indicate (IN-duh-kate)—to show or prove something

pioneer (pye-o-NEER)—a person who is among the first to settle a new land

sod (SOD)—the top layer of soil and the grass attached to it

INTERNET SITES

FactHound offers a safe, fun way to find Internet sites related to this book. All of the sites on FactHound have been researched by our staff.

Here's how:
1. Visit *www.facthound.com*
2. Choose your grade level.
3. Type in this book ID **1429601574** for age-appropriate sites. You may also browse subjects by clicking on letters, or by clicking on pictures and words.
4. Click on the **Fetch It** button.

FactHound will fetch the best sites for you!

READ MORE

Apel, Melanie Ann. *The American Frontier.* Daily Life. San Diego: Kidhaven Press, 2003.

Bial, Raymond. *Frontier Settlements.* American Community. New York: Children's Press, 2004.

Graves, Kerry A. *Going to School in Pioneer Times.* Going to School in History. Mankato, Minn.: Capstone Press, 2002.

Olson, Nathan. *Blizzards.* Weather Update. Mankato, Minn.: Capstone Press, 2006.

Steele, Christy. *Pioneer Life in the American West.* America's Westward Expansion. Milwaukee: World Almanac Library, 2005.

BIBLIOGRAPHY

Dick, Everett Newfon. *The Sod-House Frontier, 1854–1890: A Social History of the Northern Plains from the Creation of Kansas & Nebraska to the Admission of the Dakotas.* Lincoln, Neb.: University of Nebraska Press, 1979.

Laskin, David. *The Children's Blizzard.* New York: HarperCollins, 2004.

O'Gara, William H. *In All Its Fury: A History of the Blizzard of January 12, 1888, with Stories and Reminiscences Collected and Comp. by W. H. O'Gara.* Lincoln, Neb.: Blizzard Club, 1947.

INDEX